I0471024

Internet Marketing
CONFIDENTIAL

How To Spot The Lies And Scams Internet Marketers Use To Rip Off Speakers, Authors, Consultants, And Coaches

Dan Janal

Foreword by Mark LeBlanc

Internet Marketing Confidential

How to Spot the Scams and Lies Internet Marketers Use To Rip Off Authors, Speakers, and Consultants

Dan Janal

Publisher: Daniel Janal Communications

United States of America

Copyright © (2013) Daniel S. Janal
All rights reserved

LIBRARY OF CONGRESS CONTROL NUMBER:
ISBN: 978-1484065334
EAN-13: 1484065336

Printed in the United States of America by CreateSpace
Bulk purchases, please contact the author

Without limiting the rights under the copyright reserved above, no part of this publication may be reproduced, stored in or introduced into a retrieval system, or transmitted in any form or by any means (electronic, mechanical, by photocopying, recording or otherwise) without the prior written permission of the copyright owner and the publisher of the book.

The scanning, uploading, and distribution of this book via the Internet or by any other means without the permission of the author is illegal and punishable by law. Please purchase only authorized printed or electronic editions and do not participate in or encourage electronic piracy of copyrighted materials. Your support of the author's rights is appreciated.

Testimonials

I wish I had read your book before I got taken in by a lot of Internet marketers who masqueraded as wolves dressed in sheep's clothing. This book is Dan Janal at his best. He has done a superb job of covering all the issues that everyone needs to know and understand about Internet marketing truths and lies.

Lydia Ramsey
Author, "Manners That Sell"

It's about time! Dan is the real deal calling out the online "gurus." Before you spend one more red cent on a program, course, webinar or membership site, read *Internet Marketing Confidential*. It will save you money and your sanity and show you how to work on your business so it has staying power and solvency.

Nancy Fox
Author, "Network Like a Fox"

As a coach, speaker and author in the dental industry I have spoken to hundreds of dentists who are struggling trying to figure out what Internet marketing strategies really get results. Dan's book is not only a must read but the "GO TO" resource that every dental practice needs to make bottom line results decisions!

Judy Kay Mausolf
Practice Solutions Inc.

People who don't know where the pitfalls are in Internet marketing ae bound to waste money needlessly. Dan Janal's authoritative read shines the light what to watch for so you don't get ripped off. This is a fabulous resource!

Mary C. Kelly
Author, "15 Ways to Grow Your Business in Every Economy"

Internet Marketing Confidential is a revealing, no-holds-barred look at online marketing from the inside out. Author and successful marketer, Dan Janal, takes you inside a secret world full of hidden agendas, tricks and traps designed to empty your wallet faster than you could ever build an online business. But, forewarned is forearmed. Janal softens the blow by sharing what actually does work as well as how to (realistically) compete successfully online. This book is an excellent resource for all levels; a must-read for those new to Internet marketing.

Linda M. Lopeke
Chairman & CEO
Lexicorp Services Inc., Toronto, ON

"Simply put, *Internet Marketing Confidential* has blown the doors off ALL the dirty little secrets that the scammers don't want you to know about. If you're a high-integrity, high-intelligence entrepreneur, speaker, consultant or independent professional, the fact that you've come across this book will save you literally thousands - if not tens of thousands - of dollars. Dan Janal lays everything out in his insightful, easy-to-understand tips, warnings, and advice. Nothing is left out, nothing is assumed. This book could have been called *The Consumer Watchdog Guide to Internet Marketing* because that's precisely what it is - fair, balanced, and unflinchingly honest. Dan provides a powerful reality check to protect your time, your money, and your business. If you're reading this blurb and considering buying this book, my advice is simple: DO IT!"

David Newman, author of "Do It! Marketing: 77 Instant Action Ideas to Boost Sales, Maximize Profits, and Crush Your Competition"

"Dan's advice in many areas I've lived and learned from within my own businesses. This is a damn good book! Finding fact versus fiction and hype online can be a daunting task. The genius of Dan's advice is that he provides warnings to save the reader time, money and frustration, but that he also provides practical solutions and advice to use the Internet to market more effectively."

Tony Rubleski   Author, "Mind Capture" book series
MindCaptureGroup.com

"The entrepreneurial world and small business world and start-up world, all need this information desperately. It will save them so much time, so much frustration, so much waste, so much money and that's only the beginning. I wish this book would have been available $40,000 ago."

Darshan Shanti
Author, "24 Hour Champion"

"As a creator of high quality information products and services, and coming from a corporate background, I was shocked at what was being sold -- make that hyped -- in the Internet Marketing world. I can't tell you how many of my subscribers and customers have been burned by scams and inferior products. Hey, I even Include myself in that group! That's why I'm so glad my good friend and colleague Dan Janal has created *Internet Marketing Confidential.* This is, by far, the most comprehensive source of scams, pitches and failed promises I've seen to date. Even better, the book is organized and categorized so you can zero in on a precise topic with ease. Best of all, Dan goes beyond just spotlighting a scam. He shares practical advice and tips so you can become a savvy business consumer. This is a resource that belongs on every computer within easy reach. It's THAT valuable!"

Marc Harty   The "30 Minute PR Guy"
www.30minutepr.com

Table of Contents

Other Books by Dan Janal

Preface

Nearly 20 years ago when the Internet was known to only a few geeks, scientists and teachers, I wrote one of the first books to show how the Internet could be used for marketing. I was among the pioneers who had a front-row seat to the longest running show in town – The Internet Marketing Gold Rush.

Now, as Internet marketing begins its third decade, I'm taking a look at the Internet Marketing landscape and I don't like what I see.

Yes, there are a lot of good companies offering great products and services at reasonable prices. And there are many very good Internet Marketers and Webmasters offering solid advice at reasonable rates.

But there are a lot of con artists who have stolen - yes, stolen - hundreds, thousands and even hundreds of thousands of dollars from authors, coaches, consultants, hopeful entrepreneurs and, frankly, people who had no business starting a business. They thought they were galloping along the Information Superhighway but got run over instead.

In this tell-all book, I'll show you the lies, half-truths, misconceptions and downright scams that any person who wants to use the Internet to start a business or grow a business must be aware of.

As one of the more successful online marketers, I'll show what marketing tactics work as well as what to watch out for. In a follow-up book, "The Internet Marketing Blueprint" I'll show you what you can do to build and run an ethical and profitable business.

Written in the humorous, irreverent, easy-to-understand style that readers have come to expect from me, an author of six books that have been translated into six languages, *Internet Marketing Confidential* is a must-read for anyone who wants to build a business online or grow a business online.

Foreword

By Mark LeBlanc

Our world will never be the same because of the Internet. Some of us remember the days of mail and the telephone. Then we were given the gift of the copy machine, then the fax machine, the cell phone and the Internet. It's not going to stop.

Technology continues to outpace our human understanding of the potential as well as the pitfalls associated with marketing and selling on the Internet.

Dan Janal, a true pioneer of internet opportunities has seen and now shares the good, bad, ugly and the great that has now become a part of our daily lives, at work, at home and in our own small business or businesses.

This book will open your eyes, set the record straight and give you a new lens in which to make better decisions about navigating your Internet game plan.

The Internet is here to stay. It's time you look at the truth and surround yourself with the right resources that can help you sell more products and services, as well as have a bigger impact on the people you serve best.

Many people have gained and many more have lost their time and money on the Internet. You, as a buyer, have 100% responsibility in your decisions. Do your due diligence when interviewing web site designers, social media experts, and Internet marketing gurus. Ask for referrals and listen carefully to others who you can learn from. You can find people you trust and will serve you well.

There is no magic bullet or quick fix when it comes to growing your business or practice. It takes both work ethic and work effort, with a high degree of focus.

Keep in mind that even though the odds of winning the lottery are smaller than miniscule, someone always wins. There are exceptions to every rule and Dan's candor will serve the majority of readers.

The use of technology and taking advantage of the Internet are aims of every successful business owner. This book is written to prevent you from making bad decisions and will help you move forward in making something great happen in your work and life.

Mark LeBlanc
Author of *Growing Your Business* and *Never Be the Same*

How This Book Is Organized

This book is organized into four, easy-to-read chapters:

1. Lies – the lies you tell yourself.
2. Scams – schemes presented by con artists.
3. Lies – the lies Internet Marketers tell you.
4. Misconceptions – where marketers tell you only part of the story.

Read them in any order.

This isn't a step-by-step book on how to build a list or create an e-zine or design a website. There are many great books, videos and articles that you can find on Google and Amazon that will help you with the nuts and bolts.

The purpose of this book is to give you an overview of what works and what doesn't so you don't waste time or money.

Who This Book Is For – and Who It Is NOT For

This book is primarily intended to help speakers, authors, coaches, consultants and professionals (doctors, lawyers, health care professionals).

It is not intended for large businesses, national brands and very large small businesses. They play by a different set of rules because they have lots of money, lots of people are interested in their products and they have lots of people to throw at projects. They could benefit from many of the chapters here, but the information is particularly relevant to the one-person company who has an assistant or several virtual assistants and providers to run the show.

Why I'm Writing This Book and What You Can Learn

Back in 1994, nearly 20 years ago, I wrote the first book about Internet Marketing that had practical, how-to tips and tactics, as well as predictions for the future.

My books have been translated into six languages. Because of those books, I have spoken around the world – from Beijing to Budapest and all over the U.S., Canada, Mexico and believe it or not, Brazil. Even today, people have come up to me after my keynote presentations and tell me they built their businesses on the advice in those books!

It's been a long, wonderful journey!

When I spoke at University of California at Berkeley – in fact, I taught the first Internet Marketing class at Berkeley – one person asked, "Is it legal to market on the Internet?"

He said he had heard that the Internet was just a place for scientists and educators to exchange information. At that time, that was a prevailing thought.

But the world was changing.

And, boy has it changed.

Now, nearly 20 years later, companies of every size and description are represented on the Internet. Fortunes have been made – and will be made on the Internet.

But fortunes have been lost on the Internet as well.

It's not the Internet's fault.

It's the fault of con artists who have plied their ugly trade to nice people just like you.

And it's the fault of people who chase dreams built on clouds instead of on hard work and realistic goals.

You see, hardly a day goes by that I don't get a call or an email that goes something like this:

Caller: I just spent $30,000 on a website (or Google Ads, or an info marketing seminar) and it didn't do anything and now I'm broke. What can you do to help me?

Well, I can't help them build a new website or get their money back from Google or fight for a refund from a seminar company.

But I realized I can help them – and you – by pointing out the lies, misconceptions, half-truths, exaggerations, once-in-a-lifetime good luck stories and downright B.S. that stinks to high heaven so you – yes you – aren't the next person to be bamboozled out of your life savings chasing a dream spun by those thieves.

Read and learn the truth.

Why Should You Listen to Me? 100,000 Foot View

I'm the voice of reason in the sea of hype.

I've created 8 businesses that have generated six-figure sales using 8 different business models for over two decades in every kind of economic climate. Those business models include:

- Books
- Speaking
- Coaching
- Consulting
- Subscriptions
- Affiliate marketing
- Done-for-you services
- Trade show production

I've done it by under-promising and over-delivering. That's the exact opposite of what the scammers teach.

I can't guarantee you success. However, if you follow my advice then you won't get taken to the cleaners.

I'm low key, but high impact.

If you want to make a big impact, then read this book.

Disclaimer

This is not a get-rich-quick book. We make no claims to your financial success. All results will vary.

This is a how-not-to-go-broke book by not following wildly unrealistic personal expectations and by not buying products and services from shysters.

If you are a con artist, you can't sue me. I have named no names, pointed no fingers and identified no bodies. All I can say to you is go "f-" yourself and stop scamming people.

You are responsible for your actions. If you read a high-powered sales letter or see a presentation filled with psychological triggers, you are ultimately responsible for your actions. If you see these ingenious come-ons and still buy them, then you have no one to blame but yourself. You must take responsibility and stop blaming other people. If you do this, then you will have taken an important first step in never being bamboozled again.

There Are Exceptions to Every Rule

Of course everything you read here will be followed by a, "Well I know someone who did exactly that and it worked."

Yes, they did.

And, yes, you can, too.

But realize that you won't make a zillion dollars overnight.

It will take work, sometimes hard work and it will take money and it will take time.

You will make mistakes and you will waste a ton of time figuring out what works for you, in your market, at this time in this marketplace.

What worked for someone else, at a different time, in a different market might not necessarily work for you right now.

The goal of this book is to show you what has a higher probability of working and what doesn't. You'll also learn what questions to ask so you see the whole picture.

After all, one person does win the lottery.

That gives hope to all the other millions of people who lost.

You can make money on the Internet, but your chances of winning will increase when you read this book.

Don't Tar All Internet Marketers with the Same Brush

There are a great many good service providers who are Internet Marketers, Webmasters, Coaches, Consultants, PR firms, Ad Agencies and the like.

Unfortunately, there are a lot of con artists masquerading as Internet Marketers, Webmasters, Coaches, Consultants, PR firms, Ad Agencies and the like.

The intention of this book is to give the reader a good understanding of what ethical marketers do and to follow those principles – and to avoid the scammers who prey on people who have no information.

Sy Syms, the founder of the large clothing store chain, was famous for his slogan, "An educated consumer is our best customer."

My goal is to help make you an educated consumer so you make wise choices to build your business.

There are many good people out there.

Find them.

Chapter 1: Stop Lying to Yourself

"The easiest person to deceive is one's own self."

Edward G. Bulwer-Lytton
19th century British politician, poet, critic

There are two kinds of lies:

- The lies that Internet scammers tell you. This book will expose those con games and set you straight on what's real and what's not real.

- The lies you tell yourself. Those are the worst lies of all. Read this chapter to find out how to protect yourself from your own worst enemy – yourself!

Don't Lie to Yourself

Who is the biggest liar on the Internet?

You.

That's because you probably have unrealistic expectations about what can be accomplished, how much time it takes, what skills you need and how much money you can earn.

If you don't have goals with numbers, then you are lying to yourself. How will you ever know if you reach your goals if you can't measure them?

You are lying to yourself if you:

1. Believe in lottery tickets, get-rich-quick schemes and horse races. Those one-in-a-million shots are great if you are number 1,000,000. Otherwise, it's a sucker's bet. And you're the sucker. Don't be a sucker.

2. Believe that if you build a better mouse app, the world will beat a path to your door. That might have worked in the 1700's, but there's a lot more competition now. You could have the world's greatest service, product or app and you won't sell a single copy unless you tell people, convince them yours is the one they need and get them to share their credit card number. That takes work.

3. Believe that you have all the skills you need to make money. You need to master many skills or you need to hire people who have those skills. More about both those points later.

4. Believe that wishing will make it so. It takes work. Lots of work.

5. Believe that you can do this in 4 hours a week. Some businesses can operate that way, but for most of us, add 4 hours to the 8 hours you already work. Then throw in the weekends, holidays and sick days. Not a day goes by that I don't check my email – even when I'm on vacation. When your clients call, you need to be there or your business will fall apart.

6. Believe that all service providers have your best interests at heart. I wish that were so, but as you've already learned, there are people who will think of themselves first and you last. And they'll think it is your fault. Unfortunately, there are scammers and spammers all over the world and they've got your number. You must read this book and find out how to protect yourself.

7. Believe you must make a million, zillion, gazillion or bazillion dollars in order to be a success. It actually doesn't take a zillion dollars to be rich. Many people set themselves up for failure because they don't know how much money they really need.

8. Believe that more people need their service or product than really do. But if you have dreams of numbers that are unrealistic, then you will never be happy.

9. Believe that the next "bright, shiny object" will launch you to success. There's always another product, service, book, audio or video that promises you the keys to the kingdom and success that is right around the corner. Chances are that those ideas are either hogwash, overpriced, or repackaged ideas that you can get in a book for $24.95. Beware of the next big thing because it either doesn't exist or it is a rehash of some other thing.

Let's be honest:

1. How many people have built $10 million businesses? Only a handful of authors and speakers have achieved this goal. Do you have their knowledge, their following and their sense of timing to create the right product for the right audience at the right time?

2. What would you do with a $10 million business? Seriously. Can you spend that much money? Do you have a favorite charity you want to enrich? Then cool. Go for it. Otherwise, think how great your life would be if you created a business that generated $150,000 a year, every year. That's doable.

I know you.

You'd be happy making $90,000.

You'd live like a king.

Admit it.

Be real.

Be honest with yourself.

Bottom Line: You can wish for success, but if you want to achieve success, you have to work, build skills and avoid scammers.

The "I'm a Best-Seller" Lie

I'm sorry to break the news to you, but you are not really a best-selling author if you reach the top position on a subset of a subset of a topic on Amazon for one hour on one day.

A true best-selling author wrote a book that appears on a credible best-seller list (i.e. New York Times, Wall Street Journal, Business Week, USA TODAY and a few others).

You are *not* a best-selling author if you bought the books yourself.

You are *not* a best-selling author if you convinced your clients to buy the books for you on a certain day or week in an attempt to scam the best-seller lists.

You are *not* a best-selling author if you hired a company to buy the books for you.

You are *not* a best-selling author if you – and only you – claim that you are.

You are *not* a best-selling author if no one reads your books.

You are *not* a best-selling author if you have a garage full of unsold books.

You are *not* a best-selling author if you are broke.

You are *probably not* a best-selling author if the person sitting next to you has never heard of you.

You *are* a best-selling author when the books fly off the shelves today, tomorrow and for years to come.

Yes, you are allowed to market your book to make sales so you can become a best-selling author. Don't get me wrong.

But if you game the system by buying tons of books, then you are lying to yourself.

So many people call themselves "best-selling authors" without any large sales whatsoever in an attempt to sound bigger than they are. The term has pretty much lost its luster because so many wannabees claim to be "best-selling authors" but really aren't. It's like a company saying they provide "outstanding customer service."

Frankly, I don't know how they sleep at night. Maybe they think they really are best-selling authors because 100 people bought their books on one particular day. But I dare them to go up to Steven King or Danielle Steele or Ken Blanchard and say, "Hey, "I'm a best-selling author, just like you."

Bottom Line: Don't lie to yourself. People will think you are lying and will not trust anything else you say. Instead of being a best-selling author, you might be a "b-s author."

The "Everyone Needs My Stuff" Lie

I wish it were true.

And if it is, then my hat is off to you!

But first, ask yourself how you know that everyone needs your stuff?

Did you ask people who are not your friends or immediately family? They always will be supportive, even of a bad idea.

Did you conduct research?

Or did you have "gut" feeling that everyone needed this?

If the latter, are you prepared to bet your house, your savings and every spare minute of your life for the next three years on your gut?

Bottom Line: Trust the market, not your gut. The odds are better.

The "Spreadsheet Marketing" Lie

Here's the most common lie I heard people tell themselves when I was doing day-to-day publicity for high tech companies.

I call it the "spreadsheet marketing lie."

It goes like this:

"The widget market is huge. It's a one-bazillion dollar industry. If we get 1/10 of 1 percent of that market, we'll make one gazillion dollars."

The trouble is that it doesn't matter how big that market is if they don't need your product.

Do you need another spreadsheet?

Or word processor?

Or a book about your topic?

If the answer is "no," then all the time, money and energy isn't going to convince someone to buy it.

Get real.

Get real goals.

Do real tests.

Get real education.

Then hit the marketplace.

Bottom Line: Internet Marketing can't work if you have blinders on your eyes.

The "If I Could Get on Oprah, I Could Make a Fortune" Lie

If I had a dollar for every person who said Oprah could make them rich, I'd be rich.

Many people have gone on Oprah and haven't made a fortune.

Why?

1. People who watch Oprah don't necessarily want to buy your book on employee's rights or whatever you are promoting. They want to be entertained and informed. They didn't turn on the TV saying, "I hope there's a book I can buy."

2. You aren't the only person on the show. Do you think everyone is going to buy everyone's book?

3. Do you buy a book after you see someone on a TV show? No? Then why would you expect everyone else to?

4. Oprah isn't seen on as many TV sets as before. She's on her own network now, in case you haven't noticed. That network is not shown in many homes.

5. You really don't watch Oprah and really don't know what she is looking for in a guest.

Oprah has helped a few books become best sellers. That's because she believed in those books and actively promoted those books. If she loves your book, then you are off to the races. Otherwise, you are just one of 20 guests on the show that week.

Bottom Line: Nice work if you can get it. But the odds of winning the lottery are only slightly better. Buy your ticket, but don't quit your day job.

The "I Can Do It All Myself" Lie

Every speaker, coach, author and consultant I've ever met says the same thing. "I can do it all myself. Why should I hire someone?"

I admit that I suffered from that lie as well.

Here's what I realized: Just because I could design a website or balance the books, or do sales, didn't mean I was any good at it or that my time couldn't be better spent on other tasks I excelled in.

My life changed when I hired a webmaster. I didn't have to keep up with all the changes to programming languages, security concerns, Google updates and many other factors.

My life changed when I hired a bookkeeper to balance my checkbook, a task that took me 10 hours a month. She does the same job in about 3 hours and it costs me less than $150.

My life changed when I hired someone to take over sales and admin. Not only did it free up many hours, we found a surprising result: we got more clients!

There are many ways to find highly qualified help at reasonable prices. Ask your colleagues for referrals and recommendations. Test them out with a project and you're set.

Caveat: Be aware that many people could charge vastly different prices for the same service. Just because they charge more doesn't mean they are any better. I've heard a zillion stories of people being ripped off by vendors who promise the sun, the moon and the stars and charge an equivalent fee.

Bottom Line: Do your homework and find good people to do what you don't like to do, don't want to do, or who can do it better than you can.

So You Want to Be a Speaker!

Congratulations!

Some speakers are among the best-paid people on the planet.

They get handsome fees for speaking and people run to the back of the room to buy their books. They can make a fortune.

However, there's more than meets the eye.

The average professional speaker makes $50,000 a year, according to a survey by the National Speakers Association (NSA). A recent issue of NSA's Speaker Magazine contained two articles that said if you want to make a living as a speaker, you need to rely on more than speaking fees to make a living!

The world of speaking is changing rapidly. Celebrities, actors and newscasters can get tens of thousands of dollars for a speech. However, subject matter experts and motivational speakers, unless they are well known, will make less. However, they can make a good living – especially when they have multiple streams of income from speaking, coaching or consulting and selling books. Business owners use speaking as a marketing tool to get new clients and might not even ask for a fee for speaking.

Many meeting planners try to get speakers for free. They know that authors will speak for free in the hopes of selling books; consultants will speak for free in the hopes of getting clients and large companies will send executives to speak for free to help promote the company. In other words, you could have a great message and be a great speaker, but lose the gig to a person who will do the job for free.

At some conferences, speakers actually have to PAY a fee to speak!

Don't expect to leave your day job and begin making an equivalent amount of money as a speaker. It's tough to get hired; there is a lot of competition at every price level on every topic.

Speaker bureaus don't want to work with beginning speakers. They want to work with established speakers whom their clients are asking them to book.

Meeting planners don't like to be bombarded by emails and phone calls from speakers. They rely on recommendations from their meeting planner friends.

There are a zillion books, consultants, coaches and workshops that will teach you to be a speaker. Do your homework before you buy. If they sell a million-dollar dream, run for the hills. There are very few million-dollar speakers.

Bottom Line: Speaking is a very good way to get new clients. It is a wonderful marketing tool to grow a business. The money very well could be on the client side. If you want to be a speaker, be prepared to offer additional services to make a good living. Also, speaking is a great launching pad to grow a business that has multiple streams of income.

So You Want to Be an Author!

Congratulations!

Some authors are among the most respected and well-paid people on the planet. They write books and their adoring fans buy them by the truckloads at fancy book launch parties. They appear on the TV talk shows and are celebrities.

However, according to many sources, the average book sells only 500 copies! I'm not sure if that figure includes all the books sold by Steven King and Danielle Steele or not. If not, then the average book sells even fewer than 500 copies.

Of course, the con artists will point to a few success stories of unknown authors who wrote eBooks that have been true bestsellers (like "The Road Less Traveled" and "50 Shades of Grey.") However, those are the exceptions, not the rule.

Should you write a book?

Yes – if you keep your eyes open and have realistic visions.

1. You probably will not get rich from your book. If you publish with a traditional book publisher, you'll get about $1.50 for every $30 book that is sold. You don't have to be a math genius to know that you have sell a lot of books at $1.50 to make a fortune. That's not where the money is.

2. If you self-publish a book, you could make nice money and even serious money because you keep all the profits. Of course, you have to create the book and take care of all the production process and the expense.

3. Your book is a big business card. People are still impressed with authors. You can use your book as a way to open doors to new prospects and build rapport with clients. That's where the money is.

Bottom Line: Your book is a big business card that can help you get new clients for your main business.

So You Want to Be a Coach!

Congratulations!

Coaches seem to get big money for their programs, workshops and retreats. If you believe their websites, they can charge hundreds and thousands of dollars an hour!

Of course, what they print on their websites and what they really get paid could be two different things entirely!

I know a lot of coaches who teach coaches how to sell coaching programs. They describe their average client as a married woman with two kids, a Chevy Suburban, a mountain of debt from attending coaching training sessions and a husband who says, "When are you going to start making money with this coaching thing or get a real job?"

Don't get me wrong. Coaching is a great profession and you can make a good living at it. Be prepared to invest in your skills as a coach and your skills as a marketer to build a successful business.

Bottom Line: Some coaches are geniuses. Some coaches are frauds. You need to build your profile so the market can see the difference.

What It Takes to Build a Business with Internet Marketing

Let me set you straight on what it really takes to build a successful business with Internet Marketing.

1. You need skills to win. You can't expect to win if you don't know how to write sales copy, if you don't know how to network effectively, if you don't know how to ask for the order and lots of other skills. You won't win if you are afraid of technology, afraid of numbers or if you are afraid to talk to people. Fortunately, you can learn those skills by reading inexpensive books at Barnes and Noble or by taking classes at your local university extension. You don't need to know all these skills. You can hire people who can do these tasks for you. And for that, you need money. Sad but true. Let's get real.

2. You need money to win. You don't need as much you might have needed 5, 10 or 20 years ago though because the cost of computers, websites, domain registrations and other marketing services has gone down - in fact, many services are free and they are good! However, you do need money, but you don't need – and shouldn't have to – take out a second mortgage or dip into your retirement savings. Especially if you avoid scammers who will charge whatever they think they can get from you.

3. You need to have a good product, or better, a great product to win. And you have to have an audience that really, really, really wants it. Too many entrepreneurs crash and burn because they have a "great" idea that no one wants. Forget the saying, "If you build a better mousetrap, the world will beat a path to your door." First they have to know they need your product. Then they have to know you exist. That takes time, skills and money as well as a great product. They need to trust you and that takes time.

4. Finally, you need to be realistic to win. Don't lie to yourself and say, "Everyone needs one. Everyone will buy one." Do you buy every product you see advertised? Do you buy every book being mentioned in an interview you listen to? Do you see every movie listed in the papers?

Do you call every number on every ad you see advertised on TV? No? Then why would you expect your prospects to buy when they see your ads, your products and your publicity? Do you realize that direct marketers consider their marketing campaigns a success if 2 percent of the recipients of their direct mail (junk mail) result in sales? 2 percent! Why would you think your product would do any better?

5. Set a time limit and a money limit. Everyone has finite resources. Don't spend more than you possibly can afford to chase your dream. When you've spent that money or that time, admit to yourself that it didn't work and reassess. Don't throw good money after bad money. Say to yourself, "I gave it my best shot. The market didn't want what I thought it wanted. It is time to move on."

Bottom Line: Get real.

Essential "Do's" That Will Improve Your Chance for Success

Ask yourself these questions:

1. What are your goals?

2. Are they realistic?

3. Are your goals so pie in the sky, high in the sky that you are setting yourself up for failure?

4. Is there an audience for your product or service?

5. Do they know they need this? Or will you have to spend a fortune educating them or convincing them?

6. Can you do market research to see if people want your product and if you have enough money to reach them?

7. What are the results of these tests?

8. Can you live with the worst outcome?

Don't mortgage your house or your soul.

Bottom Line: Set realistic goals and you won't be disappointed. Set unrealistic goals and you'll never be happy.

Don't Beat Yourself Up!

I hope you didn't get depressed from this chapter. That's not my intention.

You can make money on the Internet and feel good about it.

I know too many people who work long hours and make some money but it isn't as much as they thought they'd make and it didn't happen as fast they wanted and it wasn't as easy as they were led to believe.

I'm here to tell you it isn't your fault.

You were misled.

Now you are going to find out what works, what doesn't work and what you can do to protect yourself so you can win.

Chapter 2: Scams

"Why are the most risky loan products sold to the least sophisticated borrowers? The question answers itself – the least sophisticated borrowers are probably duped into taking these products."

Edward Gramlich, Board of Governors, Federal Reserve

This section shows the out-and-out scams and bad tactics you must avoid at all costs.

There are bad people out there and they love to prey on people who are nice, kind and trusting.

In other words...

You.

The Scammers Blueprint

They sell you a dream.

They paint a rosy picture.

They add urgency.

They add a sense of losing out if you don't buy.

Then you're hooked.

It's a simple formula, as old as the hills and it works.

You've been misled your entire life by get-rich-quick schemes, by people who brag about how much they've made and your own inner voice telling you that the grass is greener on the other side.

Bottom Line: Know when you are being manipulated and defend yourself.

You Know They Are Lying to You When They...

... Make you feel like you are losing out on something

... Paint a picture that it so rosy and bright you can see it and taste it

... Make it sound so incredibly simple

... Make you feel like a loser now and their product will turn you into a winner

... Make you feel like a loser if you don't buy their product

... Make claims sound too good to be true

... Tell of financial claims that are unrealistic

... Make obstacles sound too easy to overcome

... Say you don't need any experience

Bottom Line: If it sounds too good to be true...

Is the Person Truly an Expert in that Field?

Premise: They claim, "Trust me. I'm an expert."

Definition: Anyone can call themselves an "expert" or a "best-selling author." But are they really?

Truth-o-meter: Some are, some aren't. Check and verify.

Discussion: You'll find lots of people selling Internet marketing courses on a variety of subjects.

You need to ask them if they got rich by actually doing the work and learning the ins-and-outs. Or did they get rich by selling materials that teach people the subject matter?

For example, did they actually learn how to flip houses, lose weight, get their life in balance, have 100 coaching clients, speak to 100 corporate conferences, and sell a zillion books? If not, how do you know they can teach you to do it?

It's the difference between reading a book about basketball and actually playing the game.

You've heard the old saying, "Those who can't – teach."

I'll improve on that bromide:

"There's more money in teaching than in doing."

Bottom Line: If you are going to spend money to learn how to market online, make sure that person has actually made a fortune doing the things he is going to teach you. If not, run for the hills and hide your credit card.

The "You Can't Afford NOT to Buy My Product" Scam

Premise: They claim, "You can always find money to buy this product."

Definition: Scammers show you how to tap into your mortgage, retirement funds and credit cards to get you to buy their products.

Truth-o-meter: This is the most brazen sales pitch I've ever heard. Run for the hills.

Discussion: I was sitting in an info-marketing seminar a few years ago and the pitchman (I dare not call him a speaker because that would cloud your image of professional speakers) was going into high gear to sell his product.

It went something like this.

Pitchman: "You absolutely have to have this product. Don't tell me you can't afford it. Don't tell me you don't have money. You have money. If you have a house, you have money. You can take out a second mortgage. If you have credit cards, you have money. Put the money on your credit cards. If you don't have enough money on one card, that's okay. You can split it up onto two or three or four cards. If you have a retirement account, you can borrow from your retirement account. This product will help you make so much money you won't even notice what you are investing in it."

Bottom Line: If you can't fund your Internet marketing venture with ready cash, then wait and save enough money so you can.

Don't Trust Anyone Who Made a Fortune and Lost It

Premise: They claim, "It's so easy to make a fortune. I've done it three times!"

Definition: The get-rich-quick industry is littered with people who made it and lost it and brag about it.

Truth-o-meter: I've heard these people speak. Run away!

Discussion: Anyone who made a fortune and lost it and made it and lost it again is not a great entrepreneur. They might be people with personality disorders.

They can't deal with success. They don't feel they deserve it. They don't know how to manage money.

I'm not a psychiatrist so I can't explain the phenomenon, but I have a pair of eyes and I can see the handwriting on the wall.

People who can't manage their money shouldn't be your mentor.

Of course, I'm not including people who lost their businesses during the recession, or had a health problem or a family issue.

Bottom Line: Sound money management is an essential step toward success. It's okay to believe in someone's rags-to-riches-story. But leave the room when they start talking about how they lost it.

The "Overpriced Services" Scam

Premise: They claim, "Our prices are high because we provide quality work."

Definition: Companies charge whatever they think you can pay.

Truth-o-meter: Be careful.

Discussion: Yes, this is America and capitalism is great. Anyone can charge whatever they want to charge. And you are free to accept or to decline their offer.

But there comes a point when people are being ripped off. There are online pirates in every industry who charge outrageous prices for their services. They prey on people who trust others and who don't know any better.

Prices and quality vary greatly. A high price does not guarantee great work. Don't get ripped off when you buy:
- Webmaster services, including web design, hosting, domain names.
- Teleseminars and webinar services. Many services are free
- Marketing services (i.e. publicity, copy writing and advertising)
- Coaching and consulting services
- Product creation, such as book printing, copy editing, layout and design

Fortunately, you can combat these villains. You need to do your homework and find what prices are fair in today's market.

Some service providers actually add more value. They are entitled to extra fees. However, make sure you need those services. Otherwise, you are being ripped or paying for something you don't need.

Bottom Line: Do your due diligence and talk to two or three vendors to get a range of prices before making a decision.

The "Link Buying Scam"

Premise: They claim, "Buy 100 links for $100 and get better listings on Google."

Definition: Links are one way to improve your site's ranking on Google, but only one of many, many ways. Companies try to sell you links to improve your visibility on Google.

Truth-o-meter: False.

Discussion: You get an email that offers you the "opportunity" to buy 100 links from other web sites for $100 and the promise that the more links you have posted on your website, the better rankings you'll get on Google.

Sounds like a low-cost way to get great visibility.

Right?

Wrong?

Google decides where to rank your site based on hundreds of factors. The links pointing to your site are one such factor. However, they rate the quality of those links. If you have links from government, education, media or other high-traffic business sites, you get brownie points from Google. If you have garbage links – like link farms in third-world countries set up to steal money from people like you – then Google doesn't count them.

Related Item: Don't engage in link exchanges. No money changes hands in this deal, but you won't get better listings on Google, either. Don't waste your time. However, if one of your networking partners offers and exchange – in other words – someone you know and trust – then you might consider exchanging links.

Bottom Line: Don't waste your money buying links.

The "Amazon Best Seller Campaign" Scam

Premise: They claim, "If you create an Amazon Best-Seller Campaign and you'll sell lots of books, get lots of attention and make lots of sales."

Definition: An attempt to get your book to rise to the top of Amazon so you can say you are a "best-selling author"

Truth-o-meter: Yes, but, but, but.

Discussion: Many years ago, a smart marketer realized two things:

There was value in saying you are a "Best Selling Author on Amazon."

There was a way to game the system.

Gaming the system was easy.

Here's why it works. Amazon has created categories and sub- categories. For example, they have a category called "Marketing." Inside that category is "Publicity." Some categories have many sub-categories. It's a great way for readers to find books they could be interested in.

The Amazon Best-Seller campaigns target those sub-categories. The more sub-categories a topic has, the easier it is to rise to the top.

That's because they are targeting a sub-list in which not many books are sold. They created a marketing plan that asked people to buy your book on a certain day (or even during certain hours on that day). In exchange for proof of purchase, the buyer would also receive hundreds or thousands of dollars' worth of eBooks, MP3s, PDFs and other digital products from well-known authors in that field.

In other words, they are tipping the scales. They are building a fire and hoping it burns through Amazon's numbers and rankings.

This tactic can work. As an experiment, I participated in a mini-version of this over New Year's Day with 20 other authors and many books became #1 on their categories. That's because very few people buy books on New Year's

Day. And fewer buy from 6-9 am Pacific Time. The system was gamed. But I doubt any books sold in any great quantities beyond that day.

But what did this prove?

Did it lead to more book sales?

Did it lead to word of mouth for the books?

Did it create massive sales and sustained growth?

No.

It did let 20 authors say they were "best-selling authors."

Frankly, I'd never be able to live with myself if I said I was a best-selling author by using that technique.

But you aren't me.

Let's say you wanted to do this. Here's what you'd need:

- $2,500-$30,000 to pay one of the high-priced consultants who engage in this kind of fiasco.

Or you can do it yourself. Here's how:

- You'll need about 100 hours of your time.

- You'd need to round up 20 or so other authors who would contribute free digital products to juice up your offer.

- You'd need to write sales copy to entice them.

- You'd have to contact them to get their buy-in.

- You'd have to follow up with them to make sure they delivered the promised material by your deadline.

You might ask why they'd want to participate. Easy. They get more publicity for their books and brands. Each digital product they give away will have ads for their products and ordering information as well as links to their websites.

Authors do want to participate. You'd want to find 20 authors with complementary books so there is synergy between the products and the markets. In other words, if your book is on leadership, find 20 other leadership authors. If your book is about knitting, find 20 authors of knitting books.

Oh yes, I almost forgot. Each author pledges to send your sales letter to their lists of followers. That's how you get large numbers of people to know about your project. Without the reciprocity in mailing lists, your project is going nowhere. Now you have to find people with big lists. After all, if your partners tell 100 people, you aren't going to get as many sales as if they told 10,000 people. You have to pick your partners strategically.

Then you have to write glowing sales copy to get people to buy the books.

And you'll have to create a page with all the links to the giveaways. People click on the links to get their freebies.

You'll have to work with the authors to make sure the links on their sites are up and working properly.

Or you can post a page to your site and have people download the files from your site.

And make sure they all work. If one product can't be downloaded easily, you'll have to field support calls from angry buyers – buyers who are angry at 3 a.m.

You'll discover some partners are easy to deal with and can post their files easily. Some partners are hard to reach, difficult to follow up with and are technical morons who find this exercise frustrating and you'll have to hold their hands. And you'll find everything in between.

After it is all said and done, I'm not sure you would have sold more than 100 books, though, so it is unlikely you will recoup your investment by book sales. You better hope your book really does capture people's attention so you get more sales after the big launch.

And you thought writing was the hard part in creating a book!

Bottom Line: You can become an "Amazon Best-Selling Author" if you have the time, energy or money to carry out the many complicated steps.

Chapter 3: Lies

"A truth that's told with bad intent
Beats all the lies you can invent."
— *William Blake*, *Auguries of Innocence*

Some people are liars.

This chapter shows you what to watch out for.

The "This Program Is Push-Button Easy" Lie

Premise: They claim, "Making money is easy. Just copy what I did – step-by-step."

Definition: Hypesters, especially technology hypesters, say this when selling a product involving technology, like a website or a copywriting course.

Truth-o-meter: Maybe if you have a degree in computer science, otherwise, plan on calling a techie.

Discussion: A television is push-button easy.

A remote control?

Not so easy.

Case closed.

Every off-the-shelf, push-button easy website or program, or app requires time to learn.

Techies can't create products that are easy to learn.

In fact, they can't even say the words "easy to learn."

They have to say, "This program requires a learning curve."

With a mindset like that, do you think they can create easy products?

Sorry.

Plan on learning some tech skills or programming skills.

Or plan on hiring someone who does.

Bottom Line: Very few things are intuitive. Put a PC person in front of a Mac and watch him tear his hair out. It isn't intuitive.

The "This Book/Course/Program/Software/ Can Change Your Life" Lie

Premise: They claim, "Read my book, or info-course. You'll get rich."

Definition: The underlying message of any sales pitch for a massively overpriced info-product or self-help program carries this message.

Truth-o-meter: The right program, at the right time, for the right person might actually change your life, but the odds are stacked against you.

Discussion: Human beings are hard-wired to resist change and to keep bad habits.

If it were easy to lose weight, stop smoking and exercise consistently, we'd all be thin and healthy.

Does that look like reality to you?

If people don't change from reading, oh, the Bible, or hearing a clergyperson deliver a talk once a weekend every weekend of their lives, do you think a paperback or a three-ring binder of ideas is going to be more effective?

Research has shown that most people who buy self-help books don't read past the third chapter (if they open the book at all). But research has also shown that those same people will buy another book and another course on the same topic. And read no further.

That's what makes humans so wonderful - and so gullible.

You can learn a new tactic, a new strategy, a new skill and that can make all the difference.

Bottom Line: You are more apt to improve by taking baby steps than by trying a massive makeover in a short period. Don't throw your money or self-esteem away by chasing unrealistic expectations.

The "Girlfriend, You Need My Info-Product" Lie

Premise: They claim, "Girlfriend, only another woman can help a woman succeed in business."

Definition: Women info-marketers pretend to be your best girlfriend to get you to buy their stuff.

Truth-o-meter: Manipulations isn't prettier if it is wrapped in pink.

Discussion: One of my women clients identified this. Women play the "girlfriend" card to get women to buy their services "for women only."

I'm sure women have different problems than men that require special training and instructions for issues men don't have. They also have a great many similar problems. But these sales pitches play on gender differences and why you should trust that person because she is a woman.

They urge you to trust your "inner goddess," "feminine instinct" and (well if I say other things, I'll be outing very specific people and I won't do that).

They use pink. (Dare we call them the "pink-collar" marketers?)

Think of pink as a warning sign that someone is playing with the emotions of your feminine mind.

By the way, in case you are cursing men for not having this problem, don't worry. Male marketers target male buyers with other sets of insecurities, like fear, greed and inadequacies.

Ripping people off is a non-gender-specific equal opportunity exploiter.

Bottom Line: Buy someone's service because it has value, not because the marketer made you feel guilty or inferior.

The "I Can Get You #1 Ranking on Google-Guaranteed" Lie

Premise: They claim, "My SEO (Search Engine Optimization) company can get you to the top of Google so more people find you. Guaranteed."

Definition: Companies send you unsolicited emails claiming they can get you to the number one position on Google.

Truth-o-meter: Don't believe them.

Discussion: This is another claim you should view with extreme caution.

No one can guarantee they can get Google to do anything. Google is too smart for that.

I've had a lot of success with getting my clients on the front page of Google and sometimes the top position – but I never guarantee it!

That's because Google decides who gets top position based on many factors including (but not limited to), the site's age, the links pointing to the site, the quality of the links pointing to the site, the internal mapping structure of the website, and a zillion other factors that Google doesn't make known.

Then there's the competition. The site that is number one got there for a reason. Do you have enough of these points covered to pass them up? In case you don't realize it, there are about 20,000 other competitors fighting to get onto page 1 of Google just like you.

Getting to the top of Google isn't easy but it can be done by reputable companies using reputable tactics. If you use a company that uses tactics that Google disapproves of, then your site could be banned from Google for years.

Yes, years.

Here's one more dagger to stick into this false claim. One of the prime laws of physics says that two objects can't occupy the same place at the same time (think of the game "Musical Chairs). The same theory applies to being number one on Google. Only one company can be there at any given time.

What makes that SEO company think they can displace another? And even if they do, how long will it take before someone knocks you out of that spot?

Bottom Line: Don't believe any company that promises to get you to number one. There are no guarantees.

The "Pitch Fest Masquerading as Educational Seminar" Lie

Premise: They claim, "Come to this seminar and learn everything you need to get started in info marketing from 12 experts."

Definition: A seminar that promises to teach you about a topic but really is choreographed to sell you expensive info products or expensive coaching/consulting programs.

Reality: The presenters whet your appetite about the topic and the riches it could provide. Then they offer to spill the beans when you buy their stuff.

They say, "I can't go into great detail in the 45 minutes they've given me to speak."

And they are right. Most speakers tell you about the dream you want to hear and the opportunities to reach that dream. But they don't tell you how to get there. It's like reading chapter one of a book. They establish the need in your mind and in your heart.

You pay a hefty fee to register for the event, fly to the site, stay in a hotel and eat hotel food. You deserve a world-class education. Instead, you are treated like a captive audience that must buy anything and everything. I've seen presenters use vicious intimidation, subtle wordplay and psychological tricks to get people to buy.

I went to a seminar just to hear one speaker, a famous info marketer. He spoke for 45 minutes and said, "They really didn't give much time to talk, so I can share only a little bit of info with you." He then gave a very little bit of info. He got a nice applause. Then the seminar promoter asked him to come back and talk about his new program. He spoke about that new program for two hours! I timed it! It was a brilliant sales job. But I felt abused.

Bottom Line: You're better off buying a book on that topic for $24.95.

The "Sales Pitch That Starts with a Snail Mail Letter and Invites You to Dinner in a Hotel" Lie

Premise: They claim, "You can make a fortune if you attend this info-event for free at your local hotel. We'll even give you dinner!"

Definition: A sales meeting to get you to buy the latest get-rich-quick business.

Truth-o-meter: They'll get rich. You won't.

Discussion: If you go to your mailbox and see an invitation to attend a marketing seminar in a hotel and they'll give you a free meal, run, don't walk to your garbage can and shred the flyer!

Don't stop.

Don't reconsider.

Don't wonder, "I bet this isn't like all the other scams."

It is.

These events are scripted to manipulate you to buy their stuff.

There is no such thing as a free meal.

A gift given demands a gift in return.

It's called the Law of Reciprocity.

They think they can buy you with a $12 dinner so you spend $4,995 on a training course.

There's only one winner in that scenario and it isn't the person who ate the rubber chicken.

Bottom Line: Shred the letter before your bank account is shredded.

The "Save Money By Hiring Offshore Workers" Lie

Premise: They claim, "People in the Philippines and India are marvelous workers and can work cheap! You can save a lot – and you won't sacrifice quality. And they speak English as well as you do!"

Definition: People in other countries work for peanuts compared to what U.S. workers charge. You'll hear many claims to save money by hiring offshore workers to write, edit and program.

Truth-o-meter: Do your homework. Every person is different.

Discussion: I've heard wonderful stories about programmers from India and other countries who do great work for low fees.

I've also heard stories of programmers in India who can't understand American English, who like to take 3-week vacations in areas that don't have Internet access and who really don't give a flying leap.

I've heard of people whose books were edited by people in other countries and they were not pleased with the results.

I've seen emails from people that read like this:
For example:

"Compliments of the day to you and do sincerely hope you are fine."

It might look like English, but it isn't.

Bottom Line: Investigate all contractors. Diligently check references and make sure the references are real.

The "Marketing Programs from Publishers" Lie

Premise: They claim, "We published knows your book and know the media. It's in your best interest to let them market your book."

Definition: Publishers of vanity press books offer to market your book – for a substantial fee.

Truth-o-meter: No way.

Discussion: When you have your book published by a newfangled publishing company, they will try to sell you a PR and marketing package. They contend that they know your book and they know how to promote it. Or they sell you a package to teach you how to market your book. Either way, you are out another $4,000. But you might not have anything to show for it because:

1. PR is hard. It takes time and money. You love your book like a baby because you worked so hard to make it happen. However, they publish 10 books a week. You are nothing special to them. And they have other books to promote as well.

2. They look after their own self-interests. One of my clients showed me a press release her publisher had written for her. It read like this:

"Our Publishing Company Publishes New Book, about Bullying"

Discussion: A proper press release would highlight the topic, the author and the book title, not the publisher.

The press release went on to say:

"Our Publishing Company, the leading publisher of works by authors, speakers, coaches and entrepreneurs, is pleased to announce today that it has published another wonderful book in a long series of wonderful books. This one is about bullying and it is by Your Name."

"We are pleased to create cost-effective solutions for authors who want to get their books published," said Joe Bigwig, president of Our Publishing Company. "As we continue to grow and expand, we offer all authors a chance to get their books published professionally and make their dreams come true."

Discussion: A proper press release would discuss the book and its key points. The publisher's background and self-serving statement are not needed in the least.

I might be exaggerating, but only a little bit. The press release was about the company, not about the book or the author.

Bottom Line: Make sure you know what you are getting in any PR or marketing program. Ask questions. Talk to other companies to see what they can do for the same money.

The "My Info Product Is Worth Its Weight In Gold" Lie

Premise: They claim, "This info product has all the answers you need to be a success."

Definition: Info Products are expensive packages of information, usually several loose leaf binders and spiral bound books, DVDs and/or CDs. They can also be books, single or double set CDs, but for the purposes of this chapter, I'm focusing on the big-ticket items.

Truth-o-meter: You can lose a lot of money when you buy info products.

Most info products selling for $500 to $5,000 and more are rarely better than a $24.95 book you can buy at a bookstore. Look for best sellers in that topic that have stood the test of time. Or look for college textbooks that might offer even greater depth and have relevant case studies, as well as questions to prompt you to think about the topic. Heck, for $5,000 you can take a college course and talk to a Ph.D. teacher!

This isn't actually a scam. It's just an overpriced product. Look for a similar book on Amazon, or a course at your local university. You could find the same information for a lot less money and lot more interactivity.

Bottom Line: Look for similar titles at the local library, bookstore or adult education class at your local university. You might find the same information for much less money.

The "Four-Hour Work Week" Lie

Premise: They claim, "You can run a successful business by working only four hours a week."

Definition: According to a popular best seller, you can do everything you need to do to become a success in just four hours a week.

Truth-o-meter: If you've already built a successful business, you might be able to spend four hours a week keeping tabs on it – while your general manager watches over all day-to-day operations. But if you are starting a business, you're going to need a lot more than four hours to build and run a business.

Discussion: There are no easy paths to building and running a successful business online.

You have to learn new skills, write lots of copy, make lots of contacts, try lots of techniques and might even have to test different businesses before you find the right one that works for you.

This takes time.

Bottom Line: The *Four-Hour Work Week* is the best title ever for a book, but it isn't the recipe to run a business if you are starting a business. If you work part time, you'll have a part-time income. This could be great news for a person who wants to raise a family by day and build a business by night.

The "Throw Up a Website and People Will Come" Lie

Premise: They claim, "If you build a website, customers will come and they will buy and you will get rich."

Definition: Advertisers show you fancy ads on TV and in magazines proclaiming you'll have a successful business if you buy their website building program.

Truth-o-meter: Why do they always use the term "throw up" when they say this phrase? Think about it.

Discussion: Well, if you don't have a website, no one will come.

That's for sure.

But if you put up a website, you still have to get people to come.

It is hard work to get people to visit a website.

What? You think your site is the only site on the web?

Far from it.

There are millions and millions of web sites from every country in the world.

Selling every kind of product you can think of.

And many of them compete directly with yours.

So if you post a website and it is absolutely brilliant (as it must be), then you have to market the site so people will come.

Those tactics can include buying ads, doing publicity, writing articles and creating videos.

In fact, you need to do just about ALL of these tactics to get traffic to your site.

It can be done.

It is being done.

Every day.

In every way.

But you must work it.

And you can never stop.

Never.

Never.

The day you stop marketing is the day that people stop coming to your site.

Don't believe me?

Look at the remainder bin of books at Barnes and Noble.

Every one of those famous authors, celebrity authors and big-name, honest-to-god bestselling authors has his or her books in the remainder bin selling for $5.

Those authors stopped marketing and started working on other projects.

Bottom Line: If you build it, they will come if you market the right service to the right audience at the right price. And you never, ever stop.

The "You Are Too Stupid to Create a Website" Lie

Premise: They claim, "Websites are too complex for you to build. You must hire a webmaster."

Definition: Webmasters want business and they will say whatever they can to make the sale – and charge whatever they can get.

Truth-o-meter: False.

Discussion: Websites were difficult to build at one time. You used to have to know how to program a website with arcane code called HTML. If you can't spell HTML, you couldn't build a website.

Then WordPress came to town. Websites can be easy to build if you use a WordPress blog. WordPress is the greatest boom to Internet Marketing since the invention of the browser.

With a WordPress blog, you can be up and running in a few hours and have a website where all the links work and the site looks like it came from a professional designer. Google will even index your site!

Now comes the hard part. You have to turn the website into a marketing machine. That means you have to create enticing advertising copy and pictures. Maybe you can do this. Maybe you will need to hire someone.

You need to capture names and email addresses so you can follow up with prospects. This isn't hard. There is software that can do this. But you have to know where to get the software, how to plug it into WordPress and how to manage the data once you collect it. Again, that's no reason not to be an Internet marketer. It is just something you need to account for.

Bottom Line: WordPress has made it easy and affordable for many people to create their own websites and should bring down the cost of creating a website if you need to hire a webmaster.

The "Websites Are Expensive" Lie

Premise: They claim, "You must spend a lot of money to create a good website."

Definition: Webmasters are free to price their services at any rate they like. You are free to say no.

Truth-o-meter: You could spend a lot of money. You don't have to spend a lot of money.

Discussion: Websites can be inexpensive. Read the preceding chapter.

I want you to be aware that if you talk to a company that produces websites, they will charge you whatever they think they can get from you.

But if you find a webmaster who knows how to work with WordPress and is honest, you can have a website built for less than $1,000 and probably less than $500.

WordPress is a game changer for anyone who wants to have a business on the Internet.

Bottom Line: You can get a fine looking website with all the tools you need for a less than $5,000. Keep asking for recommendations until you find those honest people.

The "Webmasters Can Build Money-Making Web Sites" Lie

Premise: They claim, "A webmaster can make any business a success on the Internet."

Definition: Webmasters think they know about how run a successful business on the Internet. In truth, they know how to put a business website on the Internet successfully. They might not know anything about how to run a business or conduct a marketing campaign or make money. They make art.

Truth-o-meter: It all depends on the webmaster.

Discussion: A good webmaster is worth his weight in gold.

I have a great webmaster.

That's because he has a marketing mindset.

Most webmasters can't sell a t-shirt at a rock concert.

That's because they are either artists or techies.

Artists can design a pretty site but it won't sell a thing.

Techies can create a compliant site that won't crash, but it won't sell a thing.

A webmaster who knows how to market can make you money.

Bottom Line: Find a webmaster who knows about marketing, as well as art and technology. Avoid artists and techies who can't sell.

The "Books Will Make You Rich" Lie

Premise: They claim, "You'll get a gigantic advance, your books will fly off the shelves and you'll be rich!"

Definition: This is the hope and dream of every person who ever stared at a blank sheet of paper and said, "I'm going to write a book." This is also the lie told by vanity publishers who charge to edit, print and market a book – even if they know it has no chance of success.

Truth-o-meter: It worked for John Grisham and perhaps 100 other true best-selling authors; but without constant promotion the books will not fly off the shelves. In fact, very few books sell enough copies for the author to make a living. However, you can make money when you use the book as a big business card (see that chapter) or if you doggedly pursue bulk sales opportunities at speaking events and with prospects.

Discussion: Book marketers love telling the stories of the few self-published books that were true bestsellers and were later published by true New York publishing houses. But those stories are the exception, not the rule.

Books can make you rich if you sell a lot (and I do mean *a lot*) of books. Several of my clients and friends in the National Speakers Association have sold literally 100,000 books to their clients and their speaking audiences. Also, books can make you rich when you sell additional services like consulting and coaching.

Most likely, books will make your publisher rich. The odds and profit are stacked in favor of the publisher. If the book sells for $30, you get about $1.50. That's because the publisher sells the book to the bookstore at 50 percent off. You get a 15 percent royalty on that sale. It's not a lot of money.

If you buy books from the publisher, you can sell them, of course. But you don't get the royalty. And many publishers won't sell you the book at cost – they sell you the book at the price of the bookstore. So you might pay $12 for your book and sell it for full price at your speeches. You can make money, but the margins aren't as good as you might have thought.

Bottom Line: Books can help build your credibility so more people buy your products or services. But you'll make your real money on your services (or the back end), not the book. See the discussion on "Books Are a Big Business Card" for more inspiration.

The "We Had So Many Callers, The System Crashed!" Lie

Premise: They claim, "We had so many callers for our teleseminar or webinar that our system crashed! Here's proof we are so popular, you better buy our stuff because everyone else is."

Definition: Marketers try to show you how popular their teleseminar or webinar was by sending you an email that says "the system crashed."

Truth-o-meter: False!

Discussion: This is one of the biggest lies you'll hear. And, also, one of the stupidest.

Here's how it goes.

You've signed up for a teleseminar or webinar and you didn't attend. Later that day, you get an email from the host of that event with the subject line reading, "Sorry, Our System Crashed" or something similar. The letter says their seminar was so successful, so wonderful and attracted so many more people than they ever imagined that the phone system crashed!

Don't believe a word of it.

1. If the system did crash, they'd sue the telecom provider for all the money they could have made from people who were on the call! They wouldn't be bragging about it!

2. I'd wonder what kind of experts they were if they didn't do their homework to locate a reputable teleseminar company that has a reputation for quality service!

3. A reputable teleseminar provider has ways to accommodate thousands of callers. Yes, mistakes can happen, but if it did, the Internet marketer would scream at the telecom provider.

4. They wrote these messages weeks before the seminar was held.

5. They copied a template of this letter from an Internet marketer who has no shame or ethics (neither do they!)

6. The system didn't crash.

Bottom Line: If you can't believe this message, what else can't you believe from that person?

The "Oops, I Sent the Wrong Link" Lie

Premise: They claim, "Oops, I sent the wrong link in the last email. Please read this email and click on the new link to buy my product."

Definition: This is another obnoxious email subject line that con artists use to try to stand out. This is one more way to create a subject line that hopes to get your attention.

Truth-o-meter: Scam alert!

Discussion: Would you trust an Internet marketer who is launching a big campaign but doesn't test all links? Would you want to hire that person to run a big campaign for you?

I didn't think so.

Yes, mistakes can happen and you would want to correct mistakes. But I think a person can tell when a mistake honestly occurred and when it is a deceptive ploy to trick people into opening an email.

Bottom Line: Don't fall for this trick. It doesn't inspire trust. And don't use this tactic on your clients just because you see other people doing it.

The "It's Easy to Create Content" Lie

Premise: They claim, "Creating content is fun and easy!"

Definition: Companies that want to teach you how to create info-products say it is easy to create content to help you overcome your innate fear of writing and your concern about entering into a production and marketing process you know nothing about.

Truth-o-meter: This can be true if you are a natural writer; else, not true.

Discussion: Don't let anyone kid you. It takes time to create content.

Recently, I was a guest on a podcast. I was interviewed for 20 minutes. I sent the audio to my transcriber – and I spent 40 minutes editing the file. That's not because I have a lousy transcriber – she's very good. The trouble is that the way we speak differs from the way write. Yes, you want to write like you speak, as the old saying goes, but when you analyze the way people speak, you'll see lots of incomplete sentences, lots of starts and stops and redo's. The transcriber isn't a mind reader, so she types all those words. Then you have to edit the document to make sense of it.

That was just step 1 (or step 2 if you include the live interview.)

I'll need to spend additional time turning my comments into articles and blog posts. I write very fast; I was a daily newspaper reporter. I can't give you an estimate of how much time it would take you to write articles and blog posts from your interviews.

You can't send an unedited transcript to clients. You can't sell an unedited transcript as product. Readers will think you are an inarticulate idiot. Yet I see it done all the time!

Of course, you can hire a writer to do this for you if you don't feel able. Either way, you are adding to your time, or to your expense.

Bottom Line: Content is king – and is worth its weight in gold.

The "You Must Publish Books with a New York Publisher" Lie

Premise: They claim, "New York publishers have more credibility than self-publishers."

Definition: Traditional publishers are feeling the heat from vanity publishers or "independent" publishers encroaching on their turf. By claiming they have better branding, marketing, production, distribution, they aim to sign authors who they think can make money for them.

Truth-o-meter: This is an outdated misconception.

Discussion: A few years ago, it was the truth. New York publishers (and West Coast publishers with good names) were the state of the art in the book publishing world.

But times have changed.

It is easy – and profitable – to publish your book yourself or to use a service like Create Space. There are many others that provide editing services, cover design, interior design and even distribution. All those services used to be expensive to do on your own, or better handled by New York publishers.

If you self-publish, you keep all the money from all the sales. If you work with a traditional publisher, you might keep 7.5 percent of the cover price of the book.

No wonder why many consultants, coaches and speakers write and publish their own books – and hire a consultant to do what they can't.

Some people think their clients will be impressed to see their book published by a big-name company. But the truth is that most people can't even name a traditional publisher. If that's not the case for your audience, then you have nothing to lose with self-publishing and everything to gain.

Bottom Line: There's no shame in vanity publishing any longer.

The "You Must Buy Every Version of Your Domain Name" Conundrum and the "Chinese Domain Name" Scam

Premise: They claim, "If you don't own all versions of your company name, book title and personal name on every domain, you could be the victim of people trying to take advantage of your good name."

Definition: A domain name is the name of your website. You must protect your name from people who would like to make money by profiting from your name. This also applies to company names and product names.

Truth-o-meter: Yes, but within reason.

Discussion: You might hear people tell you to buy every variation of your domain name. They could be well-intentioned lawyers who are being overly protective, or they could be people who make money selling domain names. It's true!

I spoke with trademark attorney Erik Pelton for advice. He suggested that you do get the basic domain names: .com, info, .tv and .net

"Registering at least several of them for your core branding is a worthwhile investment. It's worth it to avoid the nuisance factor and legal costs if someone wants to do something fishy," he said.

Of course there are other domains and other country domains. You have to draw the line somewhere. Fortunately, domain names are inexpensive.

He also advises people to register their names and company names on all social media sites since that is free. Even if you don't plan to use those sites, it is still a good idea to grab your name to avoid any hassles if someone else grabs your name. You can imagine the complications that could cause if people pretend to be you.

Finally, let's talk briefly about the Chinese domain name scam. You might get an email or letter saying they can register your name in China before someone else tries to. It's a scam. Don't respond. Just delete.

For information about trademarks and copyrights please contact:
Erik Pelton
Founder of Erik M. Pelton and Associates
Trademark attorney
http://www.ErikPelton.com

Bottom Line: Register your names with the top domains like .com, .tv .info and .me.

The "Facebook Likes" and "Twitter Followers" Lie

Premise: They claim, "Your popularity on social media is determined by the number of "Likes" you have on Facebook and "Followers" you have on Twitter."

Definition: It seems like every social media site publishes the number of people who "like" or who "follow" you. The idea is that if you have more followers than you must have more trust, more popularity and more influence. Companies try to sell tools to create more followers.

Truth-o-meter: A lie.

While it is true that it is a good thing to have many followers on social media, it is a bad thing if you paid a company to wage a campaign to buy "likes" or to automatically add untargeted followers.

Ethics aside, what good is it to add 10,000 followers if they don't read your material? Or if they aren't really qualified prospects?

You've wasted your time and money.

You might be wondering why someone would like or follow you if they have no real interest in you? Here's one reason.

They think that people will be impressed that they have a big following. There's a theory called "social proof" that states in part that we tend to trust people whom other people trust. If my site has 500 followers, that is nice. If my site has 50,000 followers, that's better.

Bottom Line: Having a small number of dedicated fans who are tuned in to your message is better than having a large number of people who are tuned out.

The "Email-Spam Con Artist" Lies

Premise: They claim, "Anything to get your money."

Definition: Spam is unsolicited advertisements sent via email. These messages promise untold riches, fame, health, sex, relationships and peace of mind.

Truth-o-meter: Don't believe anything that sounds too good to be true.

Discussion: Let's make this short since you probably know that anything that is too good to be true isn't true.

- There is no formula to make your body parts grow.

- You did not inherit a fortune.

- Your friend did not get mugged in a foreign country and now needs your financial help.

- You did not get an invitation to speak at an event in England – all you have to do is provide your bank information to accept the speaking fee.

- The IRS never asks for your confidential information in an email

- And finally, nothing good ever came from anyone sending an email from Nigeria.

Bottom Line: Suckers are born every day and there's a scammer waiting to take their money. Don't be a sucker.

Chapter 4: What They "Forgot" to Tell You about Marketing Tactics

"Lying is done with words, and also with silence."
Adrienne Rich, Women and Honor: Some Notes on Lying

Some people lie by leaving out the rest of the story.

They don't tell you about how much time, energy and luck you need to run a successful business.

What They "Forgot" to Tell You About Spam You Send

Premise: They claim "You can make money sending unsolicited emails to people."

Definition: Spam is an email message you send to people who you don't know and who didn't ask to receive your messages.

Discussion: If you don't open spam from people you don't know, then why would you think people who don't know you would open your unsolicited messages?

Spam simply doesn't make sense.

Don't buy lists of prospects from dubious companies. You are wasting your money.

You are also violating the Federal Trade Commission's rules against spamming and you could get a fine.

Bottom Line: Don't open spam emails from companies selling you lists of names of people to spam.

What They "Forgot" to Tell You About Testimonials

Premise: They claim, "Just make up testimonials. No one ever checks them."

Definition: Testimonials should be endorsements for a book, company or person. Testimonials are posted on websites as a way of proving social proof that the product works.

Truth-o-meter: There's more than meets the eye.

Discussion: In theory, testimonials should be golden. When they are given freely from satisfied clients, then testimonials are wonderful endorsement.

However, there are several elements that tarnish testimonials that you should be aware of.

- Some unscrupulous marketers create their own testimonials. Beware of any testimonial that doesn't include a full name and a company name. In other words, don't trust "Martha H. of Oberlin, Ohio." There's no way to find out if she exists.

- Some testimonial writers offer comments solely to get their names in front of new audiences. This is particularly true with authors. They couldn't care less if they were endorsing a dog.

- It's a well-known practice for people who ask for testimonials to offer to write a sample testimonial for the client to approve, or modify. This isn't necessarily a bad thing, but it should make you wonder about validity of the statement.

Bottom Line: Testimonials can be a great way to build credibility but make sure they are the right kind of testimonials.

What They "Forgot" to Tell You About Internet Radio

Premise: They claim, "If you operate your own Internet radio show, you'll be a superstar. If you appear on a show, you'll sell products."

Definition: Internet radio is a tool that lets you create your own radio talk show format.

Truth-o-meter: Have you ever listened to an Internet radio show? Chances are you have not.

Discussion: If you are one of the few people who has listened to an Internet radio show, did you buy a product mentioned on the show? Did you sign up for the person's list?

Case closed.

If you host an Internet radio show, do you wonder who is listening?

Have you wondered about the sound of the proverbial tree falling in a forest and wondering if no one is there, did it make any sound?

Welcome to Internet radio – where every host thinks this is the next big marketing tactic that will help them grab the gold.

On the positive side, hosting an Internet radio show will give you great experience in interviewing guests, lining up guests, creating products and sticking to a schedule. These are all admirable skills.

If you appear as a guest on an Internet radio show, you'll get invaluable experience being interviewed; preparing comments and you just might be allowed to get a copy of the show to sell. You could also create products or articles from the recordings. Some people talk better than they can write, so being interviewed could be a good way to create products and publicity.

Bottom Line: Internet radio is nice opportunity for building skills, but probably not for building income or lists.

What They "Forgot" to Tell You About Client Lists

Premise: They claim, "You can trust us. Look at the list of clients posted on our website."

Definition: A list of company's clients that is usually listed on their website as a way to build credibility.

Truth-o-meter: There may be more than meets the eye.

Discussion: Let's knock of the first, most obvious scam: companies just make up the lists and put names of famous companies.

The second problem with lists is that they could include names of clients *who were not happy!*

So, yes, they were clients. But no, you would not get a good endorsement if you called them.

That's all from the buyer side.

Let's look at this point from the side of the service provider.

A credible client list will go a long way toward building your brand.

Just be sure the clients listed are clients who would be happy to say something nice about you.

Bottom Line: Client lists can be great brand builders that create trust and demonstrate expertise.

What They "Forgot" to Tell You About Viral Marketing

Premise: They claim, "Create a video. Everyone will send it to their friends and you'll become rich and famous."

Definition: An idea so hot, everyone starts talking about it.

Truth-o-meter: The number of true viral marketing superstars is very small.

Discussion: What do these viral sensations have in common?

Call Me Maybe

Gangnam Style

The Evolution of Dance

These are very successful viral videos. Nearly every person with a computer has seen these and told their friends about it.

What else do they have in common?

They don't promote a product or service.

That's because the most successful viral videos are about fun topics. They aren't the result of a well-orchestrated, multi-bazillion dollar concept created by an advertising agency.

These are the holy grails of viral marketing – an idea that was so popular everyone wanted to tell everyone because they wanted to share something fun with their friends. Would you share a video about your dentist talking about root canals?

Well, maybe if it were funny.

Becoming a viral marketing sensation is what every company dreams of and what every company demands of their marketing company.

Sadly, it isn't easy to create a viral marketing sensation.

You have to have the right – well – the right everything. And no one can predict what tomorrow's next big thing will be.

A report from the ViralAdNetwork.net shows videos that go viral don't last more than a week or two.

And if your video does go viral, you better be prepared to pay for the additional bandwidth the video and support required. In fact, should you be successful, you better make sure you have the supporting infrastructure from the web and from your staff to handle the traffic and inquiries.

Of course, that would be a good problem to have!

Bottom Line: Viral doesn't last. If it were easy, everyone would do it.

What They "Forgot" to Tell You About Book Trailers

Premise: They claim, "Millions of people watch movie trailers and go to movies. Won't the same idea work for books?"

Definition: A video that promotes a book using the same storytelling techniques that movies use. Videos are posted on your website and on YouTube and/or other video sharing sites. The goal is to create interest in your book and make sales.

Truth-o-meter: It might work for movies, but that doesn't mean it will work for books.

Discussion: Book trailers are expensive to produce but they don't sell books because very few people watch them.

Have you?

I've seen a few. They are beautiful and brilliant. They are as wonderful as movie trailers.

But no one watches them.

Here's why.

You have to have a big following to get people to watch or do anything – including drive traffic to your book trailer. If you don't have that following, then give up now.

If you do have a big following, investigate if that's the best use of your money. How many books or widgets would you have to sell to recoup your investment?

Bottom Line: There are better places to spend your money.

What They "Forgot" to Tell You About Creating Info Products

Premise: They claim, "You can make a lot of money on info products."

Definition: Info Products are expensive packages of information, usually several loose leaf binders and spiral bound books, DVDS and/or CDs. They can also be books, single or double set CDs, but for the purposes of this chapter, I'm focusing on the big-ticket items.

Truth-o-meter: You can lose a lot of money on info products.

Discussion: One of the more famous info marketers was quoted in a book saying she lost $250,000 on info products because she timed the market wrong: she produced them at the beginning of the recession when people didn't have money to go to the conference and buy products.

Point is, there is no sure sale in the world. If you are creating info products, they cost money. Unlike digital products (MP3s, articles, transcripts, PDFs, eBooks, etc.) products you can touch cost money.

Lots of it.

- You have to create it.
- Pay people to proofread it.
- Publish it.
- Package it.
- Ship it.
- Ugh.

Yes, some people have done very well with info products, and others have warehouses full of stuff no one wants.

Bottom Line: Info products selling for hundreds or thousands of dollars are expensive to produce. If you choose to do this, make sure there is an audience for your product and that you have access to that audience. If not, you'll have a hard time making a profit.

What They "Forgot" to Tell You About Affiliate Marketing – Selling Other People's Products

Premise: They claim, "You don't need to create your own product. You can sell someone else's product and make money from them!"

Definition: This is called affiliate marketing. When you ask to sell someone's product, you are an "affiliate."

Truth-o-meter: In theory, yes, you can make money selling other people products.

Discussion: There are good affiliate programs and not-so-good affiliate programs. You must first check out these factors to protect yourself:

1. Is the product good? Don't just sell something to sell something. You have to believe in it. You have to know it is a good product and that your reputation will be negatively impacted if it doesn't work.

2. Do they pay good commissions? On a digital product, 40-60 percent is considered a good range for commissions because there are no costs of goods. If physical products like CDs or workbooks need to be created, manufactured and shipped, then those costs would make a lower commission acceptable. Companies like Amazon pay a very small commission, in the single digits. It could take a lot of work for you to make any money.

3. When do they pay you? Weekly? Monthly? Quarterly? Find out.

4. Do they pay only when you've passed a certain amount, like $100? In that case, they could hold onto your money for a long time. Find out.

5. It's perfectly reasonable for them to hold money for a certain time to pay for returns. Find out.

6. What kind of reports will you receive on your sales? Will you be notified each time a sale is made? Can you check an online sales report whenever you like? You should be able to do this easily if the company is on the level.

7. How will you be paid? By check? Via PayPal? There's no wrong answer. It is just nice to know.

8. Will they give you sales material to distribute with a code that tracks the sale to you? If there is no tracking code, you will not get credit for the sale. This is critically important.

9. Did you test the codes and links to make sure they work? You'd be surprised how many times they don't! It is all too easy for a misplaced period or dash to create a link that leads to nowhere.

10. How good looking and professional are the sales materials. (i.e. website, email sales copy, social media posts or tweets, etc.)?

11. How many other people are selling the same material? If too many people are selling the same service to the same audience, that could hurt your sales. I know one seminar company that has so many affiliates in the same marketing space that I got four invitations to the same event from four different people. Of course, a company could have many affiliates and they can all do well if they target different products to different markets.

Bottom Line: Choose your products and your markets carefully and you won't get burned and you could make money.

What They "Forgot" to Tell You About Finding Affiliates to Sell Your Products

Premise: They claim "As a merchant, you can use affiliates to sell your products and they can make you a lot of money."

Definition: Affiliates are sales people. They make money when they sell something for you. If they don't sell anything, you don't pay them anything. So, of course, having affiliates sounds like a great deal.

Truth-o-meter: The right affiliates can make you some money - if you constantly urge them to sell and promote.

Discussion: When affiliate relationships work, they are wonderful. You don't have to pay a salary, a bonus, benefits, health insurance or office space. Heck, you don't even have to interview them. What could be better?

And for the affiliates, what could be better than having a product to sell with no downside? After all, you don't have to create the product, store it, ship it or deal with returns. Of course, you do have to promote it, but that doesn't cost anything because your email is free.

Also, you can get affiliate tracking software to keep track of sales, leads, orders, returns and commissions due. It costs a pittance. The affiliate software program can even store the marketing materials your salespeople/affiliates will need to promote your products. I use this software: http://ow.ly/hRRcu

So what's wrong with this picture?

Most affiliates won't do anything.

You waste all that time and effort to recruit affiliates, train them, and create unique codes for them to track. Then when you let them know of an offer, they either don't send out the message, or their audience is too small or not interested.

Of course, not all affiliates are duds. Some will do the work and have the right audience. Then you'll make money.

Caveat: Check out the people who want to become affiliates. Are they the kind of people you'd like to represent you? If they engage in spamming, or have a shady reputation, then you're reputation is at stake. One bad affiliate can harm your reputation in a single email. It can take years to build your good name and only a second to lose it.

Bottom Line: Affiliates can make money for you. But you have to motivate them and realize that most affiliates don't produce any sales.

What They "Forgot" to Tell You About Distributing Video on Hundreds of Video Sites

Premise: They claim, "If you post your videos on hundreds of video sharing sites you'll get zillions of views and lots of business."

Definition: You pay a company to post your video to dozens of video sites so you get wide distribution.

Truth-o-meter: False.

Discussion: Quick.

Name four sites that host video.

There's YouTube, Vimeo and your site and maybe a guest blogging site a site hosted by your professional association or trade group.

But did you know there are hundreds of video sites on the Internet that will host your video for free? And some companies will accept your money to post your video to all of them.

Is this a wise move?

I'm sure some people will disagree with me, but I'd opt for the top two sites and call it a day.

Just because there are hundreds of sites doesn't mean your prospects know about them or visit them, or that they would see your video there. Most people can't name four video sites.

This tactic could be like the proverbial tree falling in the forest. If no one's there, did it make a sound?

Another key point: Google owns YouTube. Guess where YouTube videos appear on search results.

Answer: High, Very High.

Final point: Make sure you pay attention to keywords and SEO tactics in the headline and description so your video is indexed properly on Google so more prospects can find your video.

Bottom Line: Create videos. Post them on website and video sites where your prospects are most likely to see them.

What They "Forgot" to Tell You About Membership Programs

Premise: They claim, "You can make a lot of money each month by having a membership program."

Definition: Membership programs are monthly subscription services that entitle the customer to access a library of content that helps them. That information could include articles, sample documents and forms, tip sheets, transcripts from interviews of teleseminars and the like. It can also include multimedia such as video training, both live and recorded. Membership programs can also include access to the expert in one-on-one sessions, or group sessions. In some membership programs, members can share information and ask questions of other members in a bulletin board forum.

Truth-o-meter: Membership programs require a lot of work, require a lot of marketing and have high drop-out rates so you constantly have to market to get new members. But if you do it right, you can make a lot of money.

Discussion: When membership programs work, they are great. The info marketer makes money each month. The more months a client stays, the more money the membership site host makes.

Let's look at the pros and cons.

1. Membership clubs are fun. If you like producing fresh content each month, then they are fun. If you like interacting with clients and members, then this is fun. However if you hate to produce content or don't like working with clients, then they are definitely not fun.

2. Membership clubs are inexpensive to create. Software programs manage the site including passwords, hosting, library and chat functions. However, you have to create content each month or clients won't have any reason to return. If you like to write and create, that's great. If you can interview other people and create materials from them, that's great too. If you don't have an original idea and can't work with people to create original content, then this is definitely not for you! Also, if you have a message board, you need to stimulate discussion. If no one is talking, there's no reason for others to return.

3. Membership clubs are profitable. They certainly can be. After all, you are getting membership dues coming in each month. You also have to pay your webmaster to update the site, your production staff to record teleseminars and webinars and create transcripts and articles. If you do this yourself, fine. It's part of your salary. Be sure to keep track of your hours so you can see how much you get paid per hour. If you pay others to create content and manage the site, then you must deduct their fees from your top line to find your bottom line.

4. Length of membership. Here's the Dirty Little Secret that membership site sellers don't tell you: The average person drops the service after 3-6 months. That means you will make $300-$800 on a $100 a month program, which is nice money. But if you are charging $29 a month, then you'll make about $100-$180 which isn't bad but it doesn't go very far toward paying your expenses. Of course, there are exceptions to every rule. If you have a big audience and they are loyal and you do all the right things the right way, there is money to be made. But there is money and time to be lost, so be aware.

5. Full disclosure. Many people who sign up for membership sites don't realize there is a monthly recurring charge billed automatically to their credit cards. It's not your fault. You told people in big, bright, bold letters with yellow highlighting so they absolutely couldn't miss it. They miss it anyway. Then they call you to demand their money back. This isn't a deal killer. Just be aware of this.

Bottom Line: Membership sites can be profitable, but they require a lot of work to add content and attract new members – and keep them.

What They "Forgot" to Tell You About Facebook Ads

Premise: They claim, "People love to click on those cute ads on Facebook and read all about new products and services. You should advertise on Facebook."

Definition: Tiny ads on Facebook.

Truth-o-meter: Very low.

Discussion: Have you ever clicked on a Facebook ad?

Did you want to sign up for Facebook so you can see an ad?

Why would you think anyone else would, if you don't?

I don't care if Facebook thinks they will make their fortune on advertising, the payback for someone like you (or me) faces very long odds because people don't go to Facebook to look for ads.

Bottom Line: Avoid at all costs. On second thought, do the free offer if they have one and see what happens!

What They "Forgot" to Tell You About Teleseminars and Webinars

Premise: They claim, "People are desperately yearning to hear new information on teleseminars and webinars and will attend every session they sign up for and stay on the line the whole time and buy whatever you are selling."

Definition: Teleseminars and webinars are two ways to deliver content to prospects: the first via telephone; the second via computer. Both are good ways to build lists of new prospects, to build credibility and to make sales.

Truth-o-meter: These can be great tools to build credibility and build lists. But if you don't offer unique content or if you try to sell too aggressively, people will hang up.

Discussion: Let's look at similarities and differences.

Teleseminars are seminars delivered over the phone.

Webinars are seminars delivered over the computer.

Teleseminars are easy to set up and require no technology. Everyone has a phone. You probably want to create slides and handouts, but they aren't required.

Webinars are a bit more complicated to set up since you need to create slides for people to look at.

Both are effective for adding people to your lists, expose your content to more people and make sales at the event and with follow up marketing.

But, please, don't believe the hype that thousands of people were on my call or that we made millions of dollars.

I've hosted some pretty big names on my teleseminars and the sales numbers are less than spectacular.

In fact, one marketer I know and respect opened his sales figures and sales strategy at a public teleseminar. I'll share the results because this comes from someone who knows what he is doing, has a big list, and has people on his team. In other words, he has all the right ingredients in place for success.

In short, he said he spent about 10 hours creating the sales messages, the marketing messages to get people to attend the seminar and create the content for the seminar, as well as the sales messages he sent to people after the teleseminar.

About 100 people signed up for the call. 25 people showed up. A 25 percent attendee rate is average these days, but the figures keep going down as more free teleseminars and webinars flood the market.

Six people bought his product for about $150 apiece. He made about $1,000.

That's okay, but considering all the time and effort, that's not a lot.
But he didn't stop with the teleseminar.

He sent follow up messages to all the people who registered. They can listen to the recording if they couldn't attend live. Many people – including myself – do this. Who has free time at exactly the time of the event? Not many. So we listen later – if we listen at all.

Of the people who received the follow up materials, another 6 people bought the product.

Now he's up to $3,000 in sales for his efforts.

Again, this is not bad pay for about 10 hours of work, but you need to know:

- It is work.
- He made money but not a fortune.
- The system does work.

He has to do this several times a month and he's making real money.

Plus he is building the brand, creating credibility and establishing the trust that will get the people who paid $150 to eventually pay 10 times that much for bigger products or services in the pipeline – or have them buy additional products for years as they become customers for life. They are in his pipeline.

Both of those outcomes are very possible.

Caveat: If you host an event, be sure to give great content that builds trust. Too many events are turning into pitch fests and ads to buy a product or service. If you don't give good content, then people will hang up.

Bottom Line: Successful businesses were built with solid – if not spectacular – foundations. Webinars and teleseminars are two tools that will help you reach those goals.

What They "Forgot To Tell You About Seminars with Dozens of Speakers

Premise: They claim, "You can get lots of solid information in one easy setting."

Definition: In-person seminars or online events like webinars or teleseminars can feature 12 or more speakers who promise to "spill the beans" on all the "inside secrets" that helped build their "empires."

Truth-o-meter: Information will be shared, along with sales pitches.

Discussion: Who wouldn't want to hear the rags-to-riches stories of dozens of successful entrepreneurs? Who wouldn't want to hear a seminar to get even one good bit of advice that can make them see the world differently?

These types of seminars, whether in person or via an Internet connected device, can be life-changing.

But also realize that even Einstein can only scratch the surface in a 45-minute speech or a 60-minute seminar. To get the rest of the story, you need to buy their books, info courses and consulting.

There's nothing wrong with this, but you need to know this going in – with your eyes open.

These speakers aren't paid by the conference promoter. They might even have to pay their travel and lodging expenses. The only way they get paid is to sell their stuff. And they probably have to split part of their sales with the conference promoter who spent money to create an audience to attend the event.

In other words, there's a lot of impetus to get you to buy something or the speaker and conference organizer go hungry.

Again, there's nothing wrong with this. I've spoken at these events.

But you need to realize that the information – at best – is going to be a mile wide and an inch deep given the time restrictions.

Yes, these events are worth attending because:

- You can learn a lot, if not everything.

- You can meet other people who can help you.

- You can get new ideas and challenge existing ways of thinking.

- You can get one new idea that makes all the difference in how you run your business.

However, you need to be aware that:

- You won't learn everything you need to know.

- You will be pitched products and services, sometimes costing thousands of dollars.

You might consider attending seminars that feature in-depth learning – from speakers or distance learning centers at your local colleges. These events go deep on one topic and don't try to sell you anything.

Bottom Line: Events are great once you set expectations for what you will learn and what you will pay.

What They "Forgot" to Tell You About Telesummits

Premise: They claim, "You can build your lists when you join with other marketers to host a Telesummit."

Definition: A dozen or more other marketers each present teleseminars for each other's audiences.

Truth-o-meter: True.

Discussion: These can work but it takes a lot of work.

First you have to find a dozen or more content providers, convince them to participate in your program, and then get them to submit their marketing materials and offers. Then you have to post them to a website and create all other supporting pages and subscription forms. This takes a lot of time. Don't kid yourself.

Then you have to create marketing materials to attract an audience and get your speakers to send those messages to their lists as well.

Actually doing the interviews is easy!

Then you have to create the transcripts (optional) and MP3 replays (not optional since most people who sign up won't attend but might listen to the audio file.)

Bottom Line: It works but it takes a lot of work.

What They "Forgot" to Tell You About Publicity

Premise: They claim, "If you get your name in the newspaper or on TV, people will buy your products by the boatloads."

Definition: Media articles that talk about you and your products.

Truth-o-meter: Not true.

Discussion: People think that getting their name in the paper, or being seen on TV will change their lives.

But it could be true if you work it the right way.

Full disclosure: I'm a publicity guy. And I was a reporter and business news editor. And I have two degrees in Journalism from Northwestern University's famed Medill School of Journalism. So I know how things work from both sides of the journalism fence.

I tell my clients that publicity is part of the marketing program; it is not the be all and end all.

That's because – at best – publicity helps create awareness, credibility and visibility. These are important tools that can be used in your marketing campaign, on your website, in your proposals, and in your book proposals as well as any other kind of sales situation.

All that is worth a lot of money!

But people have the misguided impression that if you get your name in the media, then hordes of people will buy your stuff.

It doesn't work like that.

I'll give you an example.

You.

Let's say you hear an author interviewed on morning drive radio as you drive to do errands. It's a fascinating interview. You resolve to buy the book. But you can't do it in the car. By the time you get to the office, you've completely forgotten about the book.

Let's say you are watching a TV talk show and you hear a great comedian do her bit. Do you run out and buy her book? Or her CD? Or find out if she's playing at your local comedy club?

Let's say you get the Wall Street Journal or Business Week, or the New York Times. Do you read every article on every page? Of course not. So you might have missed the great article about a consultant who has a service that you could use.

What does this all prove?

- The next time you hear of that person, you might remember and say, "Oh yeah, I heard her on Conan. Let's buy tickets."

- The next time you see an ad for that book, you might say, "I've been meaning to take a look at that."

- The next time you need a consultant you might say, "I think I read about some guy who did something like this."

And if those people are smart marketers, they will have included copies of those media mentions in their marketing kits, websites and ad campaigns so you are more likely to buy.

One of the truths about marketing is repetition works. Most people don't buy when they hear about something for the first time. They need time to get familiar with the brand, do research and have a need. When all those factors come together, publicity has done its job to build credibility and trust to convert a prospect into a customer.

Bottom Line: Publicity is part of the marketing mix; it is not a direct link between advertising and sales. Once you realize that, you will have more realistic expectations.

The Final Word

As I was putting the finishing touches to this book, I received an email from a long-time client who asked me what was new and I told her.

She wrote, "I think your topic is a HUGE problem. I know people who are spending upwards of 30k for a program and not doing anything or getting anything back!"

I was sorry to hear that, but it only proves the main point of this book. There are scammers out there who will charge whatever they can get from nice people who are chasing a dream.

Thank you for reading this book. I hope you got a lot out of it. If you did, could I ask you a favor?

Please write a short review on my Amazon page LINK GOES HERE.

And please tell a friend or colleague about the book. No, I don't pay commissions on book sales. But you'll be doing everyone a big favor if you help your pals save money.

Also, this isn't the end of our relationship. I'll post new information on my website – http://www.InternetMarketingConfidential.com You will see what other people have written about scams they uncovered. Since this topic changes every day, I expect to see a lot activity.

Many people who read the drafts of this book asked, "You've told us what to watch out for. Can you tell us what to do? What marketing activities actually work?"

I listened to them and wrote a follow-up book called "Internet Marketing Blueprint." You can get it here: LINK TO COME.

Thanks again for reading the book.

I wish you the best of success in all you do!

Passive income isn't passive. You have to create the system to create the income.

What are people who say they are making a million dollars on the Internet doing that you aren't doing?

- They are LYING!
- And you are not.
- Do you buy everything you see?
- Then why would you expect everyone else to?

Be a partner with your clients. You can do amazing things together.

Internet Marketing changes all the time. You have to stay on top of it and keep learning.

Find and use the right measuring stick for you.

Progress towards a goal takes time.

Give yourself a timeline and a deadline.

Under promise, over deliver

Building a business is a marathon, not a sprint.

A little and a little makes a lot.

Additional Resources

Our website contains links to resources we trust. Go to www.InternetMarketingConfidential.com for info.

I welcome your comments and suggestions. Please post your info on our blog to help all readers, or send an email to me at dan@prleads.com

There are many books and articles on e-zines and e-zine marketing. I'd suggest you check out reviews on Amazon to find the best resources. Also, make sure the publication date is current. Internet marketing changes quickly and advice that is a few years old might no longer be valid.

Bottom Line: Look for up-to-date information to use the current best practices in your marketing campaign.

About the Author – Dan Janal

Dan Janal is president and founder of PRLEADS PLUS.com, a public relations service that helps authors, speakers, coaches, consultants and small businesses get more visibility and credibility so they can sell more products with greater ease.

USA Today called Dan Janal "a true cyberspace marketing pioneer" because he wrote one of the first books ever written about Internet marketing way back in 1994.

Dan is known for his pioneering work in online public relations through his books, speeches coaching. His clients have been featured in nearly every major newspaper and magazine.

Dan has lectured everywhere from Beijing to Budapest, as well as across the U.S., Canada, Mexico and Brazil. He's also taught at Berkeley and Stanford.

Dan has written six books for John Wiley & Sons and those books have been translated into six languages. Dan believes that publicity and marketing should be about getting results.

A former award-winning newspaper reporter and editor, Dan interviewed President Gerald Ford and First Lady Barbara Bush.

Discover more about Dan's publicity and coaching services at:

http://www.PRLEADSplus.com

Hire Dan Janal to Speak at Your Conference

Does your company, organization or association need to learn the latest trends in online marketing and publicity?

Dan is an inspiring and entertaining speaker who can move your audiences to take action.

Keynote Speeches:

- New trends in online marketing.
- How to make the Internet work for you.
- Internet Marketing Confidential: How to avoid being ripped off on the Internet.
- Internet Marketing Confidential: How to build an ethical business on the Internet.

Breakout Sessions:

- How to rank high in the search engines with publicity
- How to leverage your publicity to fame and fortune

For more information go to http://www.janal.com

GoldStars Speakers Bureau represents Dan Janal.

Contact Andrea Gold at andrea@goldstars.com.

Dan Janal Can Help with Your Internet Marketing

Dan Janal can help you get on the right track and keep you there.

With his coaching and consulting programs, you'll get unbiased advice, creative brainstorming and weekly accountability to help you build your business.

For information go to

http://www.PublicityLeadsToProfits.com
or call 952-380-9844

Request a no-obligation discussion to see if this service can help you

Other Books by Dan Janal

The definitive source of ideas and tactics to respond to reporters queries on ProfNet, HARO and other services

Paperback, $9.95

EBook, $9.95

Internet Marketing Blueprint
What really works to build a business for speakers, authors, coaches and consultants

Paperback, $24.95 LINK TO COME
EBook, $9.95 LINK TO COME

Thanks for reading
__Internet Marketing Confidential__

If you liked this book, please tell your friends
so we can all help protect each other.

If you can post your comments to __Amazon__,
that would help as well.

If you see other scams, please post the info to
my blog at
__www.InternetMarketingConfidential.com__
And go there to read updating information

Good luck!

Dan Janal
__dan@prleads.com__

www.ingramcontent.com/pod-product-compliance
Lightning Source LLC
Chambersburg PA
CBHW051330170526
45166CB00002B/753